WHAT ON EARTH IS A
skink
?

EDWARD R. RICCIUTI

A BLACKBIRCH PRESS BOOK
WOODBRIDGE, CONNECTICUT

Published by Blackbirch Press, Inc.
One Bradley Road, Suite 104
Woodbridge, CT 06525

©1994 Blackbirch Press, Inc.
First Edition

Printed in Hong Kong

10 9 8 7 6 5 4 3 2 1

Photo Credits

Cover, title page: © Joe McDonald/Animals Animals.
Pages 4—5: ©Joe McDonald/Animals Animals; page 6: ©Paul Freed/Animals Animals; page 7: ©Zig Leszczynski/Animals Animals; pages 8—9: ©Robert A. Lubeck/Animals Animals; page 11: ©Gregory Dimijian/Photo Researchers, Inc; pages 12—13: ©Fredrik Ehrenstrom/Animals Animals; pages 14—15: ©Waina Cheng/Animals Animals; page 16: ©Tom McHugh/Photo Researchers, Inc; pages 18—19: ©Miguel Castro/Photo Researchers Inc; page 20: ©Joe McDonald/Animals Animals; pages 20—21: ©Zig Leszczynski/Animals Animals; page 22: ©Paul Freed/Animals Animals; page 23: ©Michael Fogden/Animals Animals; pages 24—25: ©M H Sharp/Photo Researchers, Inc; page 26: ©Suzanne L. Collins & Joseph T. Collins/Photo Researchers, Inc; page 28: ©Zig Leszczynski/Animals Animals; page 29: ©Dr. Nigel Smith/Earth Scenes.

Library of Congress Cataloging-in-Publication Data
Ricciuti, Edward R.
What on earth is a skink? / by Edward R. Ricciuti. — 1st ed.
    p.   cm. — (What on earth series)
    Includes bibliographical references (p.   ) and index.
    ISBN 1-56711-096-7 : $12.95
    1. Skinks—Juvenile literature. [1. Skinks. 2. Lizards.]
I. Title. II. Series.
QL666.L28R53   1994
597.95—dc20   94-28249
                                                                    CIP
                                                                    AC

What does it look like?

Where does it live?

What does it eat?

How does it reproduce?

How does it survive?

TURN THESE PAGES AND FIND OUT!

A skink is a small, scaly reptile that looks like a cross between an iguana and a snake. It has a longish face, small eyes, and a pink tongue that shoots in and out of its mouth every few minutes.

SKINKS ARE REPTILES. THEIR BODIES ARE COVERED WITH SCALES, JUST LIKE A SNAKE'S BODY.

A skink is a lizard. Actually, skinks are a whole family of lizards. There are more than 600 different species, or kinds, of skinks. Skinks come in many different colors. Some have yellow-and-green or brown-and-white stripes. Others have blue tails. Some have red heads.

Most skinks have a tube-shaped body and have a snout that is slightly pointed. Skink tails become slender toward their tip and are covered by smooth, shiny scales. A skink's legs are short and often very small. Some skinks do not even have legs! People sometimes mistake legless skinks for snakes.

LEGLESS SKINKS ARE OFTEN MISTAKEN FOR SNAKES.

THE SCHNEIDER'S SKINK OF NORTHWEST AFRICA IS ONE OF MORE THAN 600 SPECIES OF SKINKS.

Skinks are not very large. A few are about 2 feet (61 centimeters) long but most are less than 8 inches (20 centimeters) long from their head to tip of their tail.

People often call the same animal by different names. The five-lined skink, for example, is also known as the blue-tailed lizard and the red-headed lizard.

To prevent confusion, scientists have special names for species and groups of animals. These "scientific names" are usually based on Latin or ancient Greek words. The scientific name for the skink family is "Scincidae." It comes from the Latin word *scincus* and the Greek word *skinkos*. Both words mean "lizard."

THE FIVE-LINED SKINK IS ALSO KNOWN AS THE BLUE-TAILED LIZARD OR THE RED-HEADED LIZARD.

Skinks have broad, thick tongues covered with tiny bumps. Some skinks have wide teeth that are flattened on top. Others have pointed teeth that are very sharp.

When they want to cover their eyes, most lizards shut their lower eyelid. The lid of most lizards is scaly, so when it is closed they cannot see. Many skinks, however, have a transparent lower eyelid, through which they can see. This protects a skink's eyes, even when they are open.

The eardrum of most skinks is deep within the head, connected to the outside only by a very tiny opening in the skin. Some skinks have eardrums that are completely buried on the inside, without an opening.

MANY SKINKS HAVE A PROTECTIVE LOWER EYELID THAT IS ALSO TRANSPARENT.

Skinks can be found on every continent except Antarctica. The largest number of species are found in the hot climates of Africa and southeastern Asia. They have many different habitats, or living areas, including forests, deserts, and plains. Although a few skinks can climb bushes and trees, almost all live on the ground. They burrow beneath rotting logs, rocks, fallen leaves, and into the soil. Some skinks, in fact, spend almost all their lives underground. A skink's body is well designed for living in tight places. Their pointed noses are useful for digging, and their smooth, tube-like bodies slide well through the soil. A skink's clear lower eyelids keep soil out of its eyes, while still allowing it to see.

A SAND SKINK MOVES ACROSS THE DESERT IN ISRAEL. SKINKS CAN BE FOUND IN ALMOST EVERY KIND OF HABITAT.

Because skinks inhabit so many different regions and habitats, they often live with a great number of other animals. In Africa, skinks co-exist with elephants and ostriches. In North America, coyotes and rattlesnakes are common neighbors. Skinks live with kangaroos in Australia, wild boar in Europe, and tigers in Asia.

SKINKS THAT LIVE IN RAINFORESTS SHARE THEIR HABITAT WITH THOUSANDS OF OTHER ANIMAL SPECIES.

Skinks look for food during the day. A few skinks feed on plants. They are the ones with broad, flattened teeth that are good for grinding tough vegetable matter. Most skinks, however, eat insects, worms, snails, and other small animals. Skinks that eat other animals are the ones with pointed teeth. Those teeth are perfect for grabbing and killing prey. The bumps on a skink's tongue point backward toward its throat and help it to swallow food.

A few skinks eat water animals. Keeled skinks of southeast Asia live along the banks of streams. Because they are good swimmers, they often catch and eat small crabs.

A GILBERT'S SKINK EATS A CRICKET IT HAS CAUGHT. MOST SKINKS EAT INSECTS AND OTHER SMALL ANIMALS.

Animals that hunt and feed on other animals are called predators. A great many different predators feed on skinks, including other skinks. But skinks are also hunted by red-tailed hawks, secretary birds, hornbills, roadrunners, and storks. Wild boar, peccaries, coyotes, mongooses, and some foxes also find skinks to be a tasty meal.

SKINKS HAVE MANY NATURAL ENEMIES, INCLUDING OTHER SKINKS. HERE, A SMALL SKINK IS EATEN BY A LARGER SKINK.

ABOVE: A TAIL THAT HAS REGENERATED AFTER BEING BROKEN OFF.
RIGHT: YOUNG FIVE-LINED SKINKS HAVE BRIGHT BLUE TAILS THAT ATTRACT ATTENTION.

Because they live in dark, hidden places, skinks are difficult for predators to find. If they are found, though, many species of skinks have another good defense. If a predator grabs a skink by the tail, it breaks off! Then the tail begins to wiggle. Predators often then go after the moving tail while the skink escapes.

Some skinks have brightly colored tails that invite predators to grab them. The five-lined skink has a brilliant blue tail when it is young and is most likely to be eaten by predators.

Because skinks are usually out of sight, scientists know little about the way most skinks mate and have young. However, quite a bit is known about the North American five-lined skink.

In the spring, when it is time to mate with a female, the dark head of the male five-lined skink turns red. That color is a sign to other skinks that the male is ready for mating. When the male sees another five-lined skink, he rushes toward it with his mouth open. If the other skink is a male, a fierce fight is likely.

Female skinks do not fight when charged by a male. If a female is not ready to mate, she runs away. If she is ready, she simply stays put.

THE HEAD OF THE NORTH AMERICAN SKINK TURNS BRIGHT RED DURING MATING SEASON.

A STUMP-TAILED SKINK OPENS ITS MOUTH IN A THREATENING DISPLAY.

When five-lined skinks mate, the male holds the female's neck in his jaws. Then he curls his tail under hers. He then places his sex cells, or sperm, inside her. His sperm join the female's sex cells, or eggs. This process is called fertilization. Each fertilized egg begins to develop into what will become a young skink. A developing skink, like

A FEMALE AND MALE (WITH RED HEAD) BROADHEADED SKINK PREPARE FOR MATING.

many other developing organisms, is called an embryo.

About half the species of skinks lay their eggs before their young are born. The young continue to develop inside the tough shells of the eggs until they are ready to hatch. The young of certain other kinds of skinks develop fully within the female and are born encased in a very thin sac, which they quickly break out of.

About a month-and-a-half after mating, the female skink digs a hole in the soil or a rotten log. Next she lays about 18 eggs in the hole, and then curls her body around them. Except when she leaves to feed, the female stays with the eggs at all times, guarding them against other small animals that might eat them.

Hatchling five-lined skinks are about 1 inch (3 centimeters) long. When fully grown, they can reach a length of more than 8 inches (20 centimeters). Skinks that hatch from eggs and those born alive both look like miniature adults. They receive no care from their mother and are able to survive on their own immediately.

A FEMALE BROADHEADED SKINK SITS CURLED AROUND THE EGGS SHE HAS LAID IN HER NEST.

HATCHLING FIVE-LINED SKINKS BREAK FREE OF THEIR LEATHERY SHELLS BEFORE BEGINNING LIFE ON THEIR OWN.

Skinks in general are not among the animals most in danger of disappearing. Some, however, are not common and can be found only in very few places. Two such skinks live in Florida. The blue-tailed mole skink and Florida sand skink inhabit only a few Florida counties. Even there, they can survive only where the soil is very sandy, which makes burrowing easier.

The numbers of blue-tailed mole skinks and sand skinks are decreasing. Scientists believe this is because the small areas of habitat in which they live are being destroyed. Without habitat, an animal cannot survive in the wild. Destruction of the skinks' habitat is being caused mostly by human activities, such as building homes and businesses. Florida conservationists are trying to protect parts of skink habitats so that these two rare and beautiful animals do not become extinct, which would cause them to vanish forever.

HUMAN ACTIVITIES, SUCH AS CLEARING FORESTS FOR REAL ESTATE DEVELOPMENT, HAVE GREATLY REDUCED NATURAL HABITATS FOR SKINKS.

Glossary

egg Female sex cell.

embryo The young organism developing within the egg.

extinct Vanished forever.

fertilize The union of sperm and egg that creates a new organism.

habitat Surroundings that provide an organism with space, shelter, and food.

hornbill Any of a group of large-billed birds that inhabit Asia and Africa.

peccary A pig-like animal that lives in the southwestern United States and in South America.

predator An animal that hunts and feeds on other animals.

sperm Male sex cell.

Further Reading

Bailey, Donna. *Lizards*. Morristown, NJ: Raintree Steck-Vaughn, 1992.

Ballard, Lois. *Reptiles*. Chicago: Childrens Press, 1982.

Caitlin, Stephen. *Discovering Reptiles & Amphibians*. Mahwah, NJ: Troll, 1990.

Fagan, Elizabeth G. *Rand McNally Children's Atlas of World Wildlife*. Chicago: Rand McNally, 1993.

Few, Roger. *Macmillan Animal Encyclopedia for Children*. New York: Macmillan Child Group, 1991.

Harrison, Virginia. *The World of Lizards*. Milwaukee, WI: Gareth Stevens, Inc., 1988.

Losito, Linda. *Reptiles and Amphibians*. New York: Facts On File, 1989.

Parker, Nancy W. *Frogs, Toads, Lizards, and Salamanders*. New York: Greenwillow, 1990.

Ricciuti, Edward R. *Reptiles*. Woodbridge, CT: Blackbirch Press, 1993.

Richardson, Joy. *Reptiles*. New York: Franklin Watts, 1993.

Smith, Trevor. *Amazing Lizards*. New York: Knopf Books for Young Readers, 1990.

Index